Kids' Poems

Teaching First Graders
to Love Writing Poetry

Regie Routman

SCHOLASTIC

NEW YORK • TORONTO • LONDON • AUCKLAND • SYDNEY
MEXICO CITY • NEW DELHI • HONG KONG

For Elizabeth

Acknowledgments

A special thanks to all the wonderful students and teachers in the Shaker Heights, Ohio, City School District who helped make this book possible. In particular, I am grateful to teachers Chris Hayward, Jim Henry, Kevin Hill, Karen Lum, Joyce Pope, and Robyn Schwartz who welcomed me into their classrooms and collaborated in teaching poetry writing. Heartfelt thanks go to Kevin Hill for his exceptionally thoughtful response to the entire manuscript.

I am most appreciative of my insightful editor and friend, Wendy Murray, who has the heart and soul of a poet. Wendy embraced this project with great enthusiasm and sensitivity and followed through on every aspect with great care, respect, and attention to detail. Thanks, too, to Terry Cooper for her enthusiastic endorsement and to Kathy Massaro for her bold, innovative design. Finally, thanks to my husband Frank who lovingly supported the entire project.

Cover and interior design by Kathy Massaro
Cover illustration by Laura H. Beith
Back cover photograph by Kalman & Pabst photo group
ISBN: 0-590-22734-3

Contents

The Kids' Poems

Summary of Instructional Plan for Poetry Writing in First Grade

Before you begin

- Establish a poetry corner
- Read poetry aloud

Suggested Sequence of Instruction for First Lesson

- What do we already know about poetry?
- What's an anthology? (see pages 37–38)
- Sharing kids' poems
  - Examples of what we notice and discuss
- Writing the first poems
  - Oral brainstorming with students before writing
  - Students writing independently
    - Affirming writers' efforts
    - Capturing the writing "gems"
- Sharing and celebrating

Ongoing, Self-Perpetuating Loop of Instructional Follow-up Sessions (minilessons)

- Sharing and celebrating
- Demonstrating
  - Reading aloud and sharing more kids' poems
  - Shared writing
  - Teacher thinking aloud and writing in front of students
  - Oral brainstorming (before students write)
- Writing poems independently
- Capturing gems for minilesson topics

Publishing the Poetry

- Collection and self-selection
- Creating an anthology

Why Poetry Writing?

O f all the writing I have done with first graders, teaching them to write poetry has been the most exhilarating and successful. Kids love it too; they are energized by the myriad of possibilities and the total writing freedom. Teachers love it; it's fun and easy to teach, and all kids thrive.

Several years ago, when I began teaching first graders how to write free-verse poetry, I was amazed at how creative and insightful *all* kids became. Students who struggled with forming letters and words and with writing sentences, and who found writing in school burdensome, blossomed in this genre. Free from restrictions in content, form, space, length, conventions, and rhyme, they could let their imaginations soar. Proficient writers also shone. Their choice of words improved, and their joy in innovating surfaced. Furthermore, for some students who felt constricted by the requirements of school writing (journals, letters, and assignments), poetry writing freed them up.

Kenneth was one such student. The act of writing was physically difficult for him, and the traditional process was unsuccessful. Adult expectations for handwriting also contributed to his dislike of writing. His teacher, Kevin Hill, commented on the impact of poetry writing: "With poetry, Kenneth was unleashed and his talents were all over the page." Fascinated by the world around him, Kenneth could finally use writing to express himself freely. Poetry writing gave him a creative outlet for his mature understanding of nature in a way that made him feel comfortable and successful. See "Spring," below, and "Wildlife" (see page 64).

Spring

Chirping
Chattering
Aromas
Something tells
Something to sing

—by Kenneth T. Lockwood

Other children also wrote easily and confidently, about sports, school, friends, pets, nature, likes and dislikes, their family, and what was on their minds. Their poems displayed energy, rhythm, passion, shape, and keen observation.

What's more, the voices of individual students were evident in their poems and convinced teachers that first graders could indeed write with "voice"—a personal and unique style. First grade teacher Kevin Hill comments, "I could actually hear individual students' voices. Even without the child's name on the paper, I would often know who wrote the poem."

About This Book

You, too, can experience this success with your first graders and teach every child to write with ease and joy; to have fun with language, form, and ideas; to write poems without worrying about rhymes; to get thoughts down quickly; to write with a personal style and voice.

The message I want you to take away from this book is: *You can do this.* Initially, it will require a leap of faith to trust the poems themselves and your own judgment to know how and what to teach. It can feel risky to try to teach something where there are no scripted lessons and where kids are given a lot of freedom. But the process is easy and structured, planning is minimal, and the payoff is huge. My hope is to guide you comfortably through the process and give you confidence to begin teaching free-verse poetry writing in your first grade.

Specifically, *Kids' Poems: Teaching First Graders to Love Writing Poetry* will show you how to:

* use kids' poems by other first graders (included in the second half of this book) to inspire and teach budding poets

* share and celebrate kids' poems

* think aloud and write a poem in front of your students

* do shared poetry writing by composing a poem with your students

* conduct minilessons on many elements of poetry writing, such as: choosing language carefully, experimenting with line breaks (deciding where each line of the poem ends), determining white space (space on page with no words), creating the ending line of a poem, writing with rhythm or a beat, choosing a title, and selecting a meaningful topic.

* create a poetry anthology

Advantages of Writing Poetry

The biggest advantage of teaching poetry writing to first graders is that every child feels competent and successful as a writer. Once again, some of the best poems, in fact, come from struggling writers.

Other important benefits:

- offers an easy and meaningful alternative to traditional writing forms
- extends students' understanding of poetry beyond rhyme to free verse (nonrhyming poetry)
- incorporates all five senses into the writing
- requires fewer words to create a meaningful message which, in turn, helps kids stay focused while writing
- de-emphasizes mechanics
- invites kids to write about compelling content and to capture strong feelings in a poem
- focuses students' thoughts on careful and creative selection of vocabulary
- extends and supports learning to read
- challenges students to be innovative with use of language
- inspires a love of poetry
- positively influences other forms of writing. Specifically, as first graders learn to write a poem, they are learning to:
  - experiment with language
  - select a meaningful title
  - identify a main idea
  - incorporate detail
  - use imagery
  - think about effective beginnings and endings
  - create a mood
  - express feelings with their own personal voice—all of which is what good writers do regardless of the writing genre.

Getting Started

Rather than relegating poetry writing to a one-time "unit," make it a vital, ongoing component of your reading and writing curriculum. Following are tips for launching a poetry-writing program, and keeping it thriving all year long.

Begin Early in the School Year

While any time of year works well for teaching first graders poetry writing, consider beginning the year with it. (Many of the samples from this book come from midyear and spring—before my colleagues and I realized how easily first graders could write poetry.) Put aside your doubts about what first graders can do. Because students can write a poem using just a few words or phrases, they can easily combine the act of composing (creating meaning) and transcribing (writing the words). Unlike other forms of writing, where students are expected to write a full sentence or more, poetry writing demands less writing effort, stamina, and "correctness."

Establish a Poetry Corner

Create a permanent poetry section in your classroom library. Be sure you have lots of books with free-verse poetry, not just rhymes. There is no one best list of poetry books. Consult your school or public librarian as well as other teachers for suggestions. Include anthologies from former classes (see page 37).

Read Poetry Aloud

Just about all first graders have already been exposed to rhyming poems. In fact, they expect poems to rhyme even though most published poetry books are free verse (except for picture books).

Talk about and read lots of free verse since that is what students will be writing. Point out that nonrhyming poems can also have rhythm and a beat. During the poetry writing focus, I recommend reading aloud nonrhyming poetry almost exclusively.

Beginning to Teach Poetry Writing

Teaching poetry writing so that all kids are successful requires an in-depth introduction. While the initial session will last about one hour, follow-up sessions, including student writing, may be a little shorter as less demonstrating becomes necessary. Don't worry too much about the length of these sessions. Of course, good management is a necessity, but what usually happens is that kids become so engaged (especially with kids' poems by other first graders) that they remain attentive and interested.

Lesson Framework

Typically, the whole-class session includes:

✻ **demonstrating poetry writing** (one or two of the following)
   ● **sharing and discussing kids' poems** (10 to 15 minutes)
   ● **shared writing (writing a poem together)** (10 minutes)
   ● **teacher writing a poem in front of students** (5 to 7 minutes)
   ● **a minilesson on features of poetry** (5 to 10 minutes)
✻ **brainstorming before writing** (5 minutes)
✻ **writing a poem independently** (15 to 25 minutes)
✻ **sharing and celebrating** (10 minutes)

During our introductory session, I limit the demonstration to the first one above—sharing and discussing kids' poems. It is the kids' poems most of all that will provide the confidence and models that spur budding poets into confident action. Also, for the first session, and one or more follow-up sessions, I include an informal assessment of what kids know about poetry, which helps guide my teaching.

What Do We Already Know About Poetry? (10 minutes)

For the first introductory lesson and follow-up lessons, gather the class together in the reading area or wherever you usually congregate for whole-class, shared activities. I begin by telling students enthusiastically how excited I am by what we're about to do—write poetry—but before we begin I want to learn what they already know about poetry. I say something like:

> I am so excited! We've been reading and enjoying lots of poems together. Today we're going to learn how to write poetry, and I know you will love doing it. I will be showing you lots of poems written by first graders just like you. That will help us get started and give you lots of ideas. But before we begin, let's find out what you already know about poetry. That will help me do a better job teaching you.

On large chart paper, I begin to write their responses. Every time I have done this activity with first graders, they never fail to say, "poems have to rhyme." See below for one first grade class's initial responses and how we added to the chart as their knowledge base grew.

Notes on What We Know About Poetry

Words rhyme.
The shape is different than journal writing.
Neat, clear writing
"You can get ideas from everything."
You can illustrate them.
Lots of words talking about the same thing
Can be fiction or non-fiction or maybe partly both
January 8, 1998

Words do not have to rhyme.
Writing can go down the page.
You don't have to have rhythm.
It doesn't have to be a song.
It could be about your "special thing."
Sometimes the sentences are long and stick out.
Use describing words.
January 15, 1998

Use question marks and "interesting dots" to make it look like a poem.
Poems can change over time.
You take a breath when you come to a mark.
When you see . . . " you slow down.
In one kind of poem, the first letter of each line tells a message (acrostic poem)
When you choose your words, they have to make sense.
Poems have white space.
Poems can start with one thing and jump to another thing.
February 19, 1998

by the smart first graders in Mr. Hill's class

Sharing Kids' Poems

(15 minutes)

During this first lesson, we move quickly from talking about poetry to reading and discussing poems by kids. By sharing kids' poems, the message is: "Kids just like you wrote these poems. You can write poems too." I want to dispel any notions about writing being constrained, hard, or requiring strict conventions. I want kids to write with ease and joy, and seeing kids' poems is the best way I know to accomplish that goal. Or, as one first grade teacher put it, "They don't see themselves as poets till they see other children as poets."

I want students immediately to see and hear that a poem:

- can be about anything
- can use few words
- has a unique form and shape
- may or may not have rhythm and a beat
- ends with a punch
- has a title

- may use invented spelling
- lets us know the poet
- is easy to create
- may be serious or humorous
- usually expresses important personal feelings

I read aloud and show at least five or six kids' poems. Until you have your own collection, start with the ones in the second half of this book. These poems are written by students just like yours—students who excel in school and students who struggle, students who like to write and students who avoid it. These are first-draft poems, thoughtfully conceived and quickly written with minimal revision. Our purpose is for students to discover the fun and joy of writing.

What Do You Notice?

As I read aloud each poem, I show the original handwritten draft. Often I read a poem twice. On the second reading, I may show the final, published copy as well.

I like to make overhead transparencies of the poems so that students can see them clearly. I want them to notice that many of the written words use invented spelling, that the handwriting is not perfect, that the poem has a shape, that it is about something important to the writer. I want them to get the message: "You can do this too."

If students are gathered around close to you, reading directly from this book can also work well. After reading the poem, I ask students, "What do you notice? What did the writer do?"

We often comment on many of the following as we are noticing and discussing the whole poem:

- topic
- word choice
- expression of feelings
- rhythm
- shape
- line breaks
- title
- ending line
- special or missing punctuation

While I used to begin slowly, introducing one element at a time, I quickly discovered that students easily take in the whole of poetry at once, and that, in fact, they write better when we discuss all the elements together. Rather than overwhelming students, "seeing" the poem as a whole seems to help them internalize the essence of poetry as a unique genre.

In the succeeding weeks, we work on individual elements as necessary. For example, once students have written a poem they like, we may focus on a title or ending line or experiment with line breaks and white space (see minilessons, pages 33–36). These focus lessons are always in the context of reading and writing a whole poem.

Examples of What We Notice and Discuss

I read Christina's poem, "Skating" (see page 40). Jason notices how Christina uses action words like "curve," "jump," and "twirl." Sarah says she likes "I am leaping through the sky." I comment on what a great line that is and ask if she is really "leaping through the sky." I ask students what Christina might mean by those words. We talk about how writers can use words that paint a picture and show how

they feel. I also ask the kids if they notice any words Christina has repeated. Several mention the repetition of "I" and "A." I say I like the way the repetition makes the poem sound.

I note the great beat and energy of the poem, how you can tell how much Christina loves skating, how she is very specific in mentioning all she does: "a camel, a sit spin, a toe loop, a half flip, a split." I ask them, "What has she done with the last line?" We talk about how "I have the whole world at my feet" is longer than other lines, that it shows her wonderful confidence while skating, and that it's a lovely ending for the poem, how the poem wouldn't sound right if it ended with the previous line: "I do a split."

I say, "How many of you have a sport that you love? Well, you can write about that in a poem."

I read "New School" by Gabrielle (see page 46).

Regie:	Listen to how the poet feels about going to a new school. [After I read the poem, we look at it and talk about the words and shape.] What words does Gabrielle use that tell us what she's feeling?
Raquel:	She's "nervous" and "scared."
Regie:	And how does she tell us how nervous and scared she really was?
Mark:	She says her "heart was beating fast."
Regie:	Yes, and that's a wonderful way to express it. She doesn't just say she's nervous and scared. She's so scared that her "heart was beating fast." She chooses her words carefully to say exactly how she's feeling. Well, we all feel nervous and scared sometimes. That's something you can write about too.
Stephan:	Last week my heart was beating fast when I got up to bat and there were two outs. I was scared and nervous I'd make the last out, and my team would lose.
Regie:	So you know just how she felt. Maybe you'll want to write a poem about that, as Gabrielle did. How do we know Gabrielle was pleased about being at a new school? She wasn't just scared. How else was she feeling?
Merinda:	She says everyone looked at her like she was special.
Regie:	Yes, and I love the way that ends her poem. She starts out feeling scared but she also feels special being in that new school.
	What about the poem's shape? What do you notice? When you write a poem you can put the words on the page the way you want them to look and sound. Does her poem look like a journal entry? How many words are on each line?
Bryan:	Some lines have one word and some have two.
Regie:	Right. Look at how she wrote it out that way on the page. Christina did the same thing in her poem. Poets think about how they want the poem to look and sound. They keep rereading the poem as they are writing it to make sure it's exactly the way they want it.

I read "My Cats" by Cecie. (see page 58).

Regie: Notice what Cecie has done. She's written about something very important to her in just six lines. Poems can be short. You don't have to write a lot. I'm going to read the poem again.

> **My Cats**
> Two cats
> One hangs
> One runs
> One dies
> One left
> I miss that skinny fellow.

What do you notice?

Josh: It sounds like Christina's "I curve, I jump." Both poems have two words on some lines.

Matthew: And she repeats "One" four times.

Regie: Good noticing. How does it sound with repeating "One?" Read those lines with me: "One hangs, One runs, One dies, One left." I love the rhythm she creates, the way she goes back and forth about those two cats. Say it with me , and let's clap it to hear the rhythm. [Regie points to words as all read and clap together—four claps]

How is Cecie feeling? Why do you think she wrote this poem?

Natasha: Her cat died and she misses him. She's feeling sad.

Regie: Yes. Notice her last line, "I miss that skinny fellow." Say it with me and clap the beat [all say line while clapping—three claps]. How many of you can tell the poem is over? Yes, it sounds like it's ended. Her last line and beat are different, and it sounds just right. The last line finishes Cecie's message.

Many of you have pets and you can write about them. Perhaps something sad has also happened to you. A poem can be about anything at all or any kind of feeling.

We continue along in this way until we have read and "noticed" five or six poems. We are now ready to write. Students have seen and heard poems about sports, family, friends, and animals. We have talked about topic, space, shape, rhythm, word choice, and endings. I tell them again, "These poems were written by kids just like you. You can write poems too."

It's worth noting that even though I rarely mention titles (unless they are significant in some way), kids hear and see the titles in kids' poems, and almost all include a title when they write on their own.

The Influence of Peer Poets

The most powerful aspect of reading and discussing poems by other kids of similar ages is the unspoken message these quickly drafted poems send to readers and listeners: "You can do this too." While teacher demonstration and shared writing are also strong models (see pages 24–26 and 29–32), the most influential models are the actual poems their peers have written. As you develop a collection of kids' poems to use from year to year (remember to save original drafts, with kids' permission), you'll find that students delight in recognizing the poems of older siblings and siblings' buddies, or poems about familiar school life.

Notice the influence of Cecie's poem "My Cats" on James who writes "Gershwin" about his dog who died (see page 60). While James has been inspired by Cecie's subject matter, he creates his own unique pattern and form.

Notice, too, how Noah, in his poem "Vinnie" has been influenced by Cecie's pattern, "One hangs, One runs, One dies, One left" when he writes about his friend Vinnie, "I run, he runs. I won, he lost." (see page 48).

Christina's poem "Skating" inspired Alex to write "Never Give Up" about his love of hockey (see page 44). Modeling Christina's poem, Alex describes what he does in detail using "I" to begin many lines and he also changes the rhythm and form at the end of the poem as she does. But he adds his own refrain, "Whew!" to the end of each stanza (grouped arrangement of lines), which expresses his feelings of great effort—as well as relief—for his increasing competency in hockey. Notice, too, that his title "Never Give Up" (instead of a simpler "Playing Hockey") conveys a permeating spirit of striving to do his best.

Kenneth's nature poem, "Wildlife" (see page 64), inspired other classmates to write about nature. Note Nathan Bixenstine's poem, "Sliding Through the Forest."

Wildlife

rippling of water
animals hunting
rustling of leaves
camouflaging
hiding from predators
bugs creeping across
the forest floor
predators surprising prey
Mother Nature slowly getting extinct
because of man

—Kenneth Peters
Bloomfield

Sliding Through the Forest

Sliding through
the forest
down
a hill
so quiet
you can't
hear it.

If
the prey
can
see
the copper
hour glass shape,
that's the only
way
it can get
away.

by Nate Bixenstine

Sometimes teachers worry when students imitate another poet's style. However, for some students such imitation provides necessary support and structure while learning the craft. For example, "Sports" by David is a close adaptation of Miriam Moore's poem "Sports" below. Eventually, students feel confident enough to create poems that reflect their own unique personality and voice. David quickly moved to writing poems in his own style after his beginning success imitating another student. Remember, too, that it's natural for any writer to be influenced by another's work; writers themselves often mention authors who have influenced their work.

Spots
A Basskltball
bouhsis. a bassball
hits. A foot ball
throes. and tehhis
ball flis.

by Miriam
moore.

SPORTS
Baseballs Hit,
Footballs Throw,
And
Tenesballs Flips

by David Yang

Writing the First Poems

S tudents have been immersed in hearing, noticing, and discussing free-verse poems and are now ready and excited to begin to write on their own.

Oral Brainstorming With Students Before Writing
(5 minutes)

Oral brainstorming of topics before students begin to write ensures that most students will get started quickly and easily with their own writing. However, when we are just introducing poetry and our sharing and discussing have taken up to thirty minutes (or more) as previously described, we may skip oral brainstorming of topics and get directly to writing. This is a judgment call. You want to keep kids' enthusiasm and energy high. With a thorough introductory lesson, most students will have lots of ideas.

For those students who don't yet have an idea to write about (usually just a few students), walk around and briefly conference with them one-on-one to help them get started. Once you have zeroed in on a topic with them, do some oral brainstorming as modeled below.

For follow-up poetry-writing sessions—after the first one—I usually do some oral brainstorming before sending kids off to write. Rather than asking every student what he is going to write about (which is time consuming and allows for only a brief response), I will ask several to talk in detail about what they think they might like to write a poem about. With the whole class "listening in," I talk with the poet. These one-on-one conversations encourage each student to pursue a topic he/she is interested in, and to think about word choice, beginnings, endings, and so on.

Here's an example of how it goes:

Regie: Who knows what they're going to write about?
Rhaniyyah: My baby brother.
Regie: What do you want to say about him?
Rhaniyyah: All he does all day long is cry, cry, cry.

Regie:	I like the rhythm of that 'cry, cry, cry.' You can put that in your poem. What else does he do?
Rhaniyyah:	He drinks a lot.
Regie:	Tell me about that.
Rhaniyyah:	My mom says he's a greedy baby because he drinks a lot.
Regie:	I'm going to write that down for you so you don't forget it [writes it on a Post-it™ and leaves it on her desk]. I love that word 'greedy' which tells how hungry he really is. Poets choose their words carefully, just as you did.
	What else does your brother do besides cry?
Rhaniyyah:	He scratches and twists and wiggles and burps.
Regie:	Wow! I like all those words you used. You chose active words that describe exactly what your brother does. Put all that in your poem. You might want to repeat some of those words the way you did with 'cry.' Okay, so how could you start your poem?
Rhaniyyah:	Cry, cry, cry, cry and drink, drink, drink.
Regie:	I love that. 'Cry, cry, cry, cry and drink, drink, drink.' It has a great, active rhythm. Everyone, let's say it together, and clap the rhythm. [We do it as a class.] Okay, Rhaniyyah, I think you're ready to start writing your poem.

My Baby Brother

Cry, cry, cry, cry
and drink, drink, drink.
My mom calls him a
greedy baby
because he drinks a lot.

I love my brother.

Scratch, scratch
twist, twist
wiggly little
baby.

Laugh, laugh
Burp, burp, burp
happy
Little baby.

(See Rhaniyyah's completed poem, "My Baby Brother" on page 78.)

Writing Poems Independently (15-20 minutes)

After we have had one or two more similar conversations about topic and word choice, I tell them something like the following:

> *Write about what really matters to you, whatever you have strong feelings about. Read your poem over to yourself to see if it sounds right. Speak the words aloud softly to yourself so you can really hear how it sounds. Think about how you want your poem to look on the page as you write it. Have fun writing. If you finish one poem, start another.*

I let them know that we'll have about fifteen minutes of "quiet" writing and those who want to share afterwards can. I also tell students to put their name and date on each poem so we have a permanent record of their work.

Students go back to their seats (or writing places) to begin their poems. Almost everyone settles down and gets to work. As they do when writing in other genres (forms of writing), kids quietly share ideas and help one another with spelling.

Affirming Writers' Efforts

As students begin to write, I circulate about the room, and briefly talk with each student, kneeling down so I am at eye level. My main purpose here is to encourage, support, and affirm each writer's efforts. Sometimes, if a student is having difficulty choosing a topic to write about, I may need to have a brief one-on-one conference.

The following comments are typical ones that I make as I meet with students. Usually, I make one such comment and move on.

❋ I like that title. I know exactly what your poem will be about.

❋ I like the way your poem looks on the page. I can tell you're thinking about that as you write.

❋ You seem to be having trouble getting started. Let's think together about the poems we looked at today. I know you have a [pet] too. You could write about that. I'll help you think about how to begin.

❋ What an interesting topic! I can't wait to see how your poem turns out.

❋ I like the words you used. I can picture exactly how you were feeling.

❋ I can see you're thinking about the rhythm in your poem.

As I walk around the room, I am always amazed at the quality of some of these first attempts at poetry. One student, who is smart but has a hard time working independently, writes a poem about her favorite plaything. In looking through her journal I see that this poem is, by far, her best content and neatest writing. It always fascinates me that when kids care about their topic, they usually take more pride in the actual transcription.

Capturing the Writing "Gems"

As the class begins to write—as well as during oral brainstorming and one-on-one conversations—when a child says or writes a "gem," I take note and make sure the class does too. I write the gem on a Post-it and leave it on the student's desk (as I did for Rhaniyyah's, on the previous page) or I will ask the writer to read aloud what he's written to the class.

For example, during the first poetry-writing session in Kevin Hill's class we want students to hear good examples immediately so, as we walk around the room, encouraging students, we are on the lookout for such gems. When we find them, Kevin or I ask kids to stop writing and to listen and look at what a classmate has done well, whether it is the whole poem, the title, the beginning lines, the rhythm, or a well-chosen phrase.

After a student stands up at her desk and reads her writing aloud, I often hold up the poem, read it again, and comment on it—its shape, particular words, the topic and title as I did after Meghan read "Panda" (see page 50).

> *What a beautiful poem! I love the words Meghan used writing about the panda: "Black mask face." That word "mask" really gives us a picture of the panda's face. And I like the feeling of slow movement in "moving slowly through China." I can picture the panda going along slowly and "eating bamboo." I also like the one word title, "Panda." That tells us right away what the poem is about.*
>
> *Look how Meghan has written her poem with the lines getting shorter just like the bamboo shoots get shorter with the panda eating them. She's thought about the shape of her poem. And I can tell she's reread this to get it just right because look where she's crossed out and added some words. That's what good writers do. They read the poem over and over again to see if it looks and sounds exactly they way they want it. Good for you, Meghan. I also like the way you used what you've been learning in science and put it into a poem.*

Once poetry writing is in full swing, after several lessons and sessions, I do not interrupt the flow during poetry-writing time to celebrate gems. But while students are in the process of writing in a new genre, this immediate sharing serves several purposes:

- ✸ congratulates the writer for her choice of words
- ✸ encourages the writer to continue to carefully consider word choice, shape, title, and so on
- ✸ serves as a model for other students; sets expectations for quality
- ✸ reaffirms students' abilities to write poetry
- ✸ gives budding poets ideas and inspiration
- ✸ builds students' confidence

Sharing and Celebrating

(7 minutes)

After the sustained writing time, students are invited to share their poems. Because poems are usually fairly short, sharing time goes quickly. All students get a chance to read their poems aloud if they choose to do so.

Sometimes, students will stand at their tables or desks and read their poems. Other times, we gather as a class in the reading-writing-sharing area, and each student reads his or her poem in the "author's chair." Some days we pair up or read in self-selected, small groups.

The purpose of the sharing is to celebrate students' efforts. I point out only what the writer has done well. Sharing the poem congratulates the writer, affirms his efforts, serves as a possible model for other students, and encourages the writer to continue writing. When the writer reads his poem, we also clearly hear the voice of the poet. At times, students instantly appreciate the quality of a poem and spontaneously applaud. Sometimes, to generate conversation, I'll ask: "What did we learn about the poet that we didn't know before?"

There is little critique during sharing time. Once again, our purpose in writing poetry is to free kids up to write, to make poetry writing fun and easy, to play around with language, to write without concern about "correctness," and to give everyone confidence in their abilities as writers. For all of that to happen, our focus must remain on honoring children's writing efforts. Our first poetry-writing session (and all sessions) end with this celebratory sharing.

Supporting Budding Poets: Ideas for Follow-up Sessions

After the first poetry-writing session, plan to focus on teaching poetry writing for at least several weeks. Such immersion allows lots of time for multiple demonstrations as well as lots of opportunities to write and share poems. To create time for this poetry focus, you may want to "set aside" other writing you usually teach.

Poetry writing follows the format of a writing workshop:

❋ demonstration or minilesson (5 to 15 minutes)

❋ sustained writing (15 to 25 minutes)

❋ sharing and celebrating (5 to 15 minutes)

Time allotments will vary and will depend on the time of year, your purposes, and the needs and interests of your students. For example, at the beginning of first grade, the shortest time frames would be appropriate.

While all aspects of a writing workshop (as well as shared reading and shared writing) are integral to poetry writing, they are not discussed in detail in this book. For full description and guidelines, see my book *Conversations: Strategies for Teaching, Learning, and Evaluating* (Heinemann, 2000).

Adding on to the "What We Know About Poetry" Chart

Once students have had some success writing poetry, consider revisiting the chart, "What We Know About Poetry." Gather the class at the beginning of a poetry-writing session, and add to or revise the original brainstorming list on chart paper (see page 10). Talk about what you now know that you didn't know before. You can repeat this activity, later on, as we did. Or once students are very familiar with writing poetry, you may want to do a shared writing to make a final chart to serve as an ongoing, visible guide for writing free verse.

Demonstrating Before Each Poetry-Writing Session

Ongoing demonstrations—5 to 15 minutes—are necessary to ensure that students have ideas for writing, expectations for quality, an understanding of the elements of poetry to apply to their own work, and the knowledge and confidence to write independently. As well, continue to read free-verse poetry aloud for the same reasons.

Demonstration at the beginning of your poetry-writing session may involve one or more of the following or any combination of these, depending on your purposes:

* sharing and noticing more kids' poems

* whole-class shared writing

* the teacher thinking aloud and writing in front of students

* a minilesson on aspects/elements of poetry

Many of these demonstration lessons arise in response to what kids are already doing or attempting to do. (The elements taken directly from students' poems create a loop of instructional content for continued strategy development. See "Summary of Instructional Plan," page 4.)

Sharing and Noticing More Kids' Poems

At the start of the writing session, share several poems by first and, perhaps, second graders. (See *Kids' Poems: Teaching Second Graders to Love Writing Poetry*) and ask students what they notice.

Use kids' poems to talk about such elements as:

* choosing a title that conveys what a poem is about (or that purposely does not reveal the topic/main idea)

* using just the right word to say what you mean

* expressing a feeling by using other words that let the reader know, such as "my heart was beating fast" (see page 46)

* creating the rhythm of a poem

* experimenting with line breaks and white space

* trying ideas for the ending line—how it may break the pattern, and how it lets you know the poem is ended.

Use "Sharing Kids' Poems," (pages 11 to 16) to guide your own lessons. When deciding what to focus on, whenever possible take your lead from the students' poems. Even though you will be discussing specific text features, treat each poem as a whole.

Whole-Class Shared Writing

Once students have heard and "noticed" some poems by other students and have had a chance to write their first poems, we write one together in a shared writing. Shared poetry writing opens up and reinforces possibilities for content, form, and language use and is therefore a recommended demonstration for the second poetry-writing session and additional follow-up sessions. In shared writing, the teacher does the actual transcription (writing of the words), so that students are free to focus on content and meaning. While the teacher and students compose collaboratively, the teacher acts as coach and scribe while guiding students to create a meaningful poem.

An Example of a Shared Writing

Here's an example of how it goes. It is our second poetry-writing session in Kevin Hill's class, it is pizza day in the lunch room, and Kevin suggests we write about that. We spend a few minutes orally brainstorming words to go with pizza and students say the following: pepperoni, peppers, cheese, sausage, tomato sauce, spicy, hot, delicious, crusty. We write these words on a chart.

Regie: Who has an idea about how we should start our poem? [calls on Jermaine, who has his hand raised.]

Jermaine: Pizza, pizza

Denise: We love pizza

Regie: Let's hear how that sounds. 'Pizza, pizza, we love pizza.' Sounds good. Let's clap that to hear the rhythm. Say it with me. 'Pizza, pizza, we love pizza.' Okay, I'm going to write that down [writes words while verbalizing word parts slowly and stretching out the sounds]. Now, read it with me. 'Pizza, pizza, we love pizza' [points to words as all read].

Regie: What kind of pizza do you like? Think about the words we just brainstormed and try to keep the rhythm and beat. Who has a line?

Marion:	Spicy pizza
Tom:	Crusty pizza
Aja:	Hot pizza
Regie:	Okay, let's try that. 'Pizza, pizza, we love pizza. Spicy pizza, crusty pizza, hot pizza.' How about if we say, 'Spicy pizza, crusty pizza, hot pizza too.' That keeps the beat. What do you think?
Nathan:	It sounds good. I like it.
Regie:	Okay, watch me write it. [writes as three lines, verbalizes sounds while writing]. Read it with me.

> *Pizza, pizza*
> *We love pizza.*
> *Spicy pizza*
> *Crusty pizza*
> *Hot pizza too.*

Regie:	Let's read it again and clap the beat. How about if we try it without "pizza" after "spicy," "crusty" and "hot" and see how it sounds.

> *Pizza, pizza,*
> *We love pizza.*
> *Spicy*
> *Crusty*
> *Hot.*

Marcy:	It sounds better.
Regie:	I think it sounds better too. How many prefer this second beat? [More than half the class raises their hands.] I'm going to cross out pizza at the end of those lines. That's what writers do when they change their minds. Read with me. [All read poem together.] Okay, do we want to add the kinds of pizza we eat?
John:	Pepperoni
Regie:	[writes it] What else?
Sam:	Cheese
Regie:	Okay, let's read it from the beginning. (All read together) What can we say with cheese to keep our beat? How about if we try 'cheese and sausage?' Read it with me.

> *Pizza, pizza,*
> *We love pizza.*
> *Spicy*
> *Crusty*
> *Hot.*
> *Pepperoni*
> *Cheese and sausage*

Elena:	I like it. You can clap the beat.

Regie: How can we end it so it sounds like the poem ends? Let's read it again and see what might fit. [All read together.]

Kevin: [teacher] How about if we say "Pizza day at last?"

Regie: Let's say it with that ending line, "Pizza day at last." [All read together.]

Carl: I like it. Let's keep it.

Rachel: It's a good ending.

Regie: [slowly stretching out the sounds and verbalizing as she writes the line] Okay, great. Let's read it all together now.

> *Pizza, pizza*
> *We love pizza,*
> *Spicy*
> *Crusty*
> *Hot.*
> *Pepperoni*
> *Cheese and sausage*
> *Pizza day at last.*

Regie: We've read this poem over and over as we were writing it. Be sure you do the same thing when you are writing so that your poems look and sound just the way you want them.

More Poems from Shared Writing

For more examples, see the following poems "We Love Hats," "Outside Our Window," "MLK, Jr." Notice that shared poetry writing can be a great way to connect what has been learned in social studies and/or science.

Kevin Hill's students wrote "MLK, Jr." as one way to organize and express information they had learned. Notice on the next page how Kevin organized thoughts from oral brainstorming before writing. (He transferred the handwritten brainstorming chart to typed sheets as a reference for students.) Afterwards, many students went on to write their own poignant poems about Martin Luther King. See "Martin Luther King" by Matthew Michael Licina, on page 52, for one example.

Martin
Luther King
He is special.
He solved problems.
He made people happy
and
he made countries
equal.
— Matthew Michael Licina

WE LOVE HATS!

SOFT HATS,
HARD HATS,
PARTY HATS,
WORK HATS,
FLOWERED HATS,
TEAM HATS.

WE LOVE HATS!

OLD HATS,
NEW HATS,
BORROWED HATS,
MADE-BY-ME HATS.

WE LOVE HATS!

STORY HATS,
MEMORY HATS,
KEEP FOREVER HATS.

WE LOVE HATS!

Mrs. Pope's Class
September 27, 1996

Martin Luther King, Jr. (handwritten chart)

$10\frac{1}{3}+1=11\frac{1}{3}$

Martin Luther King, Jr.
Special, led marches
a great man, famous
changing laws for people
  because they weren't fair
helped people — always think first
~~they~~ a peaceful solution to
  bad laws   born Jan. 15, 1929
              killed Apr 4, 1968
kind, freedom, ~~like~~ wants non-violence
leader, hero, dreamer
Speaker; didn't like fighting
Nobel Peace Prize Winner
Rosa Parks, buses
White Only   used his words
Colored   not his ~~he~~ weapons

MARTIN LUTHER KING

Nobel Peace Prize	special
helped people	famous
changing laws for people	kind
because they weren't fair	hero
a peaceful solution to bad laws	leader
a great man	speaker
wants non-violence	freedom
used his words, not his weapons	
always think first	
led many marches	

*Kevin Hill transferred the handwritten brainstorming chart
to typed sheets as a reference for his students.*

M. L. K., Jr.

A famous man
Who led many marches
To help people be free.
Powerful leader and speaker
Who changed unfair laws.
A kind hero
Who worked for non-violence and
Won the Nobel Peace Prize.
He was a special thinker!

the *Dream Believers*
in Room 1

The finished class poem

OUTSIDE OUR WINDOW

Wet leaves,

Bald trees,

Giant jaws,

Scooping piles,

Flashing lights,

Beeping sounds,

Loaded trucks,

Driving autumn away.

Mrs. Pope's Class
October 23, 1996

Shared poetry writing

Questions and Prompts
That Guide Kids

When engaged in a shared writing with students, questions and prompts such as the following are helpful for guiding (not dominating) shared writing of poems. You may want to keep these prompts, or similar ones, handy until the language becomes automatic for you:

- What should we call our poem?

- Who has an idea of how we can begin?

- What could our first line be?

- How else can we say that?

- Let's hear how that sounds with what we have so far.

- How about if we say it this way?

- Do you like the rhythm? Let's clap it together to hear the beat.

- What about an ending line?

- Let's read it trying different endings.

- Who has another idea?

- Which ending do you like best?

- Does the poem look the way we want it to? How might we change it?

- Let's read it again and hear how it sounds. Does it sound right?

- Does the title make sense?

- Do we want to change anything to make our poem look or sound better?

Teacher Thinking Aloud
and Writing in Front of Students

If you have never written in front of your students, take the risk. It will pay big dividends. Your thinking aloud and writing will inspire your students and teach them. You only have to write a little better than they do for them to take something away from your writing.

When I am writing in front of students, I try to keep my poems on a level comparable to what most students are able to do. I choose a topic that resonates for me, and yet is one that has possible connections for students' own writing. Other than thinking about what I might write, I do no preplanning for this writing. I want to remain authentic in my demonstration; that is, if I am asking students to write "on the spot," I need to do the same. (Such demonstration writing also has the advantage of not creating extra "take-home" work for teachers.) I think aloud throughout the demonstration so that kids get a clear sense of the composing process.

One day, early in the school year, I wrote about hating peas because I was forced to eat them when I was growing up. I chose this topic because it's about parents making you do something you don't want to do (a topic everyone can relate to); I want kids to know you can express your feelings in a poem; and I feel very strongly about this topic. (I love all vegetables except peas!)

Here's how I begin:

> *You know kids, when I was growing up, my parents wouldn't let me leave the table until I'd eaten all my peas. I hated peas and used to swallow them whole rather than chew them. How many of you have had to do something or eat something you didn't want to? Or, perhaps you've been embarrassed about something. Well, you can write a poem about that.*

Regie: [sitting on a chair in front of a chart tablet with the class seated alongside on the floor]. Okay, how do I want to start? Hmm. I think I'll say "When I was growing up, I had to eat all my peas." I'm going to write that down and think about where I want the line breaks to go as I'm writing. The line breaks tell you where you want your voice to stop. The line breaks also make the white space on the page, the space where there's no writing. Let's see, do I want to say, "When I was" [pauses] "growing up," or "When I was growing up"? I like keeping it all together. I think it sounds better.

I think I'll call my poem *Eating Peas*.

	When I was growing up [says each word as she writes title and first two lines]
	I had to eat—I'm going to stop at the end of this line [rereads title and first two lines]
	ALL my peas [writes and says each word]. Why do you think I capitalized *ALL*?
Mariah:	You said it louder.
Regie:	That's right, because I couldn't leave one single pea on my plate. I want to emphasize that, and capitalizing a word is one way to show that. When you write a poem you can make it look however you want on the page.
Regie:	[continuing to think out loud and write] *I still hate peas.* Okay, I'm going to read it again and see if it's exactly the way I want it.

> **Eating Peas**
> When I was growing up
> I had to eat
> ALL my peas
> I still hate peas.

Regie:	The last line doesn't sound right to me. It doesn't sound like the poem has ended. It sounds flat, as if the poem should keep going. I'm going to add "today" to the end of the last line. "I still hate peas *today.*" That sounds better. And I'm putting an exclamation mark here [today] to show I feel strongly about this. Okay, read the poem with me now. Let's hear how it sounds.
Class:	**Eating Peas** When I was growing up I had to eat ALL my peas I still hate peas today!
Regie:	I think that does it. I like the rhythm of the last line now and how it closes the poem.

After we finish reading my poem, I ask them, "Who knows what they're going to write about?" Samantha talks about being disappointed. After weeks of looking forward to visiting Grandma, the trip was canceled because Samantha's mom had a cold (Grandma had suffered a stroke and couldn't have sick people around her). We compose the first several lines together on the overhead (a shared writing between teacher and student with the class "listening in").

> **Missing Grandma**
>
> Last week
> I couldn't see my grandma
> I was sad.

Then everyone takes their seats and begins to write. I am struck by how easily most of them write and how much more settled the class seems compared to an earlier visit. Joyce Pope, their teacher, notes, "When kids are successful at what they do, they stay engaged and focused."

Teacher Writing and Shared Writing (12 minutes)

What follows is an example of a whole class demonstration that involved both teacher writing (5 minutes) and shared writing (7 minutes) before students went off to write. First, I wrote "Finally!" Then we wrote "Mother's Day" as a shared writing (see page 32).

When I wrote "Finally!" I only knew I'd be writing about the arrival of spring weather and shedding my heavy jacket after weeks of cold, damp weather. (It's typical in Cleveland, Ohio for cold weather to linger till early May.) Here's how "Finally!" evolved.

Notice how quickly and easily the poem gets written. If you choose a topic that's currently important to you, you will experience success.

Regie: I'm so excited. Finally, I came to school today with no jacket! I got so tired of wearing my winter coat in May. Okay, I want to write about that. Let me think how to start:

Finally! I like that for a title [writing on chart paper].

I woke up, [verbalizing the words and writing the next few lines]

I looked outside.

I checked the weather report. The forecaster said, "sunny and warm." I'm just going to write

Sunny and warm. That sounds right to me. I don't need to say, "The forecaster said sunny and warm." That wouldn't sound as good. Besides, in a poem, I choose only the words I need for my message. I'm going to reread from the beginning to notice how my poem looks and sounds so far [rereads]. I want to add "No extra clothes" because I was so happy to not even have to wear a sweater.

NO EXTRA CLOTHES. I'm writing that in all capitals because I really mean to emphasize it and want to say that line louder. I'm going to read it from the beginning [reads all]. It still needs an ending line.

Finally! I think that sounds right, and it sounds like the poem is over. Read it with me. [All read together.]

> Finally!
>
> I woke up,
> I looked outside.
> I checked the weather report
> Sunny and warm.
> NO EXTRA CLOTHES.
> Finally!

We move right into shared writing. I say, "Mother's Day is coming up. Let's write a poem together. You may also want to write a poem about Mother's Day."

Regie: Tell me what you do for your moms on Mother's Day.

Shawn: My dad and I make breakfast.

Regie: How many of you do that for your moms? [More than half the students raise their hands.] Okay, how about if we start *We wake up and make breakfast.* [Class enthusiastically approves of the line.] What do you make her?

Maya: Toast

Regie: [writes and repeats] *Toast.*

James: Orange juice

Regie: [writes and repeats] *Orange juice.*

> ### Mother's Day
>
> We wake up
> And make breakfast,
> Toast
> Orange juice
> Coffee
> Pancakes
> Eggs
> Bacon
> Bagels
> Waffles
> Muffins
> Apple juice
> Coffee Cake
> And a whole lot more.
> And then . . .
> We take her out to dinner.
>
> By the smart first graders in Room 1.

Notice how our list continues to evolve naturally. (As part of the writing process, several times we stop and reread our growing list together to hear how it sounds.) After "coffee cake" (with more hands still raised for suggestions), I say, "How about if we say *And a whole lot more?*" [lots of nods of agreement].

Regie: And then what happens?

Matthew: We take her out for dinner. [Everyone laughs at the humor and truth of Matthew's statement.]

Regie: [writes] *And then…*
We take her out to dinner.

Regie: I love it. You can tell the poem is over, and this ending changes the pattern and brings a humorous close to the poem. Okay, now let's read it together and see if we like the way it looks and sounds. [All read together.]

Minilessons

Minilessons can take place any time during poetry writing. With minilessons, keep in mind that the purpose is not to break apart the poem into skills or parts but to strengthen the poem and increase writing possibilities and quality. In "Examples of What We Notice and Discuss," on pages 12–14, each discussion of a poem focuses on the elements, but always in the context of the whole, meaningful poem. For example, when noticing and discussing Christina's poem, "Skating," we talk about topic, word choice, ending lines, showing feelings, and repeating words—all at once. And again, when discussing Gabrielle's poem, "New School," we talk about choosing words carefully to express a feeling, rereading a poem as you write, creating the shape of the poem, and how the poem looks and sounds.

When you are pointing out features of a poem, just look at each poem and see what you notice. What you focus on will evolve naturally from what the writer has done. Even if you have never taught this before, you will be successful.

In addition to the following minilesson ideas, examine kids' poems—in this book and in your classroom—and see what you and your students notice.

Topics

Possible choices for topics have been discussed throughout these pages. Relook at the poems in the table of contents and observe that first graders write about all aspects of their life. A topic can be light and playful, as in "Bubbles," or weighty and serious as in "My Parents Are Separated." What is important is to encourage your students to write about things they really care about. Until you have your own collection of kids' poems, you may want to begin by discussing the topics of poems in this volume.

Short Poems

I want kids to see that poems don't need to have lots of words. Especially for students who find the act of writing burdensome, such knowledge is freeing. So I deliberately share short poems (and write short poems as I did with "Eating Peas,") as a demonstration before writing and ask kids what they notice.

On the next page are two short poems by first graders to share with your students. David was a second language learner; Max struggled with eye-hand coordination. Poetry made writing to communicate possible for them. See also "Spring" on page 5 and the poetry section of this book for more examples to share: "Vinnie," "My Cats," "Panda," and "Bubbles."

Sports

Baseballs hit
Footballs throw
And
Tennis balls flip.

—by David Yang

My Friend

He moved,
He was my best friend.
Life is not easy without him.
It's Sam.

—by Max Wolff

List Poems

A list poem is easy for most kids to do, and many teachers like to begin here. Notice Bridget's list poem, "Animals," right. Influenced by her prior knowledge of poetry and by the list poem written by the class, she wrote her own list poem right after our shared writing of "Mother's Day."

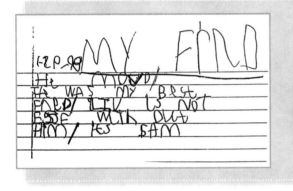

Animals

Lion
Snake
Leopards
Oh no
Lizards
sea turtle
moose
Oh no
things are scary
you know

—by Bridget Frantz

Line Breaks and White Space

Line breaks help to set the rhythm of the poem as well as to create the white space and shape of the poem. As you look through kids' poems with your students, notice the many different ways students have arranged their poems on the page: from one or two words on a line to two-to-five line stanzas.

It's been interesting to observe that young writers do not have difficulty understanding and applying the notion of line breaks and white space. In examining more than one hundred drafts of poems by first graders, almost all of them are written on the page with the shape of the poem (created by the line breaks) evolving during the original writing. Note that this statement is true for the poems included in this book. I believe that students easily grasp the notion of line breaks and white space because they have heard, seen, noticed, and discussed many poems together before attempting to write on their own.

However, when students write without line breaks, as Max did in "My Friend," on page 34, I teach them how to think about and apply the line breaks. Most often, I will say something like this:

> *Think about how you want your poem to sound and look on the page.*
> *I'm going to read your first line. Do you want it to sound [this way] or [that way]? Should we end it here or there? Which way sounds better to you?*
> *Put your line break there.*

Max added line breaks during our editing conversation. You and your students might wish to compare Max's draft to his final, typed poem.

Sometimes, Kevin Hill will type the words of a student's poem, have the student cut the phrases and words apart, and show the student how to manipulate the phrases and words into lines that look and sound the way the student wants them to. Kevin tells his students, "Put the words in lines based on the flow of your voice. Where your voice stops is the end of the line." Next, the student pastes the words and phrases, spaced as determined by the student, onto a blank sheet.

Kevin often does this exercise first with the whole class. He makes an overhead transparency of a poem from a shared writing, cuts the poem apart, and—using the overhead projector—says the words and places the words and phrases different ways until most of the class is satisfied with the resulting line breaks, white space, and shape of the poem. Kevin notes that this exercise is also powerful reinforcement of self-editing because students really do have to read every word.

Finally, there is no one "right way" to teach about line breaks and white space. What we want is for students to develop their own ear for rhythm and eye for visual form so they are able to determine what sounds and looks right to them.

Ending Lines

Beyond what has already been discussed throughout these pages, here are a few more kids' poems to use with your students when exploring ending lines:

※ "Bubbles" by Jayson Michael Douglas and "Football" by Keenen John Atkinson, page 62 and page 42. Notice how both Jayson and Keenan use the ending line to change the rhythm and shape of the poem and bring closure. Observe, too, that Jayson has crossed out his first written ending line, "That's the bubble" and changed it to "No more bubble"—an indication of his rereading, rethinking, and realizing the ending line needed revision.

※ "Vinnie" by Noah Echols, page 48. Notice how Noah uses the ending line "I never laugh at him" to show his friendship and empathy for Vinnie who has difficulty keeping up with him.

※ "My Parents Are Separated" by Tess Rose Kepner-Kraus on page 56. Discuss how the last line "It's hard making a new house your own" changes the mood of a painful family conversation and brings closure by declaring the seeming finality of the situation.

Repetition

Repeating words, phrases and lines can add much impact to a poem, as has been discussed. Here are a few more examples of repetition to share:

※ "Only One" by John Paul Gordon on page 54. Talk about how this poem is divided into stanzas with each ending "I hate being the Only One" and how that repetition lets us know the depth of the poet's feelings.

※ "Grandma" by Katrina Forman on page 70. Katrina not only begins each stanza with "Who is the one...?" she ends each with "Grandma" on a line by itself.

Careful word choice is another good minilesson focus. Use the following poems to discuss how unique language can create images, mood, and depth in a poem: "Wildlife," "My Family Likes," "My Brothers," and "A Pattern of My Favorites." Notice that careful word choice combines beautifully with inventive structures in these poems.

Publishing the Poetry

K ids love seeing their work in print. It tells them that their writing matters, and it serves as a record of their success. Because the act of writing is a big effort for first graders—who are learning to compose a message and transcribe letters and words at the same time—I recommend word-processing their poems for them. Some students will be able to manage this "final copy" work—carefully editing, handwriting, or word-processing their own published copy. Most, however, will be delighted to have an adult "publish" the completed poem for them. Not having to rewrite and work on editing and spelling keeps the joy of writing alive.

Although it is certainly not necessary to create a poetry anthology, kids love doing so and it provides a keepsake of student work. Anthologies become a favorite part of the classroom library and serve as models for creating future poems and anthologies.

Examining Anthologies

As part of one of our demonstration sessions, I begin by asking kids if they know what an anthology is. Usually, they do not. I slowly show samples of poetry anthologies—commercial and student made—and pretty soon, with some teacher prompting, someone says that an anthology is a collection of poems. I let students know we will be creating our own anthology, for the classroom library and for them, with individual copies for each student to keep. I ask them to examine these anthologies to see what they notice and like.

After students have had several days to look through anthologies on their own and with peers, we gather together and make a chart of what an anthology might include. Here's a summary of a shared writing from what one group of first graders noticed (with some teacher prompting):

- cover and title
- illustrations
- table of contents
- acknowledgments
- dedication
- poets' photographs
- information paragraph about each poet
- index

Creating an Anthology

Once students know what an anthology can include, we decide as a class—through another shared writing—exactly what our poetry anthology will contain and how it will be organized. For example, students in Kevin Hill's class decided to include an "About the Poet" page just before each published poem page. See below for a student's page and Kevin's page, which served as a model for his students.

Including one poem from each student, or allotting one page per student which may permit two short poems, seems to be most practical. Having students select a poem or two also serves as a form of self-assessment. Most teachers expect students to write at least several poems over the course of our focus on poetry writing. Now they are asked: Why did you choose this poem? Why is it your best?

Teachers note that often the poem a student selects is not the one they would have chosen. Kevin Hill notes that while his choice would be based on fluidity of language and description, kids' choices are usually based on the topic most important to them. Kids go for meaning and personal significance.

The anthology you create can be as simple or as complex as you choose. There is no one right or best way. Do what you can comfortably manage and enjoy. Do make individual copies for each student to keep and treasure. As Kevin says, "The anthology is a mirror of your class—the personalities, interests, the writing styles, and language abilities."

FIRST POEMS
OF
FIRST GRADE

written and illustrated
by
the First Graders of
Room 1,
Boulevard School
1995-96

About the Poet

Mr. Kevin Hill

Mr. Hill goes to visit his friends in New Hampshire every summer. He loves the mountains around Lake Winnipesaukee. While living there before moving to Ohio, Mr. Hill saw two bull moose on separate occasions as they were crossing the road. ("Why did the moose cross the road?") Mr. Hill loves his class this year and wants them to remember the many times they all laughed together.

25

About the Poet

Cecie Culp

I have a cat and his brother already died. I chose this poem because I want to remember my cat, Franky. I learned to write better in first grade by writing harder words. I would like people to remember that I care about the world, the environment, and, especially, the animals.

15

Closing Thoughts

While the purpose of this volume has been to inspire you and your students to write poetry, the connection between reading and writing is too important to neglect. Student poems are often used for shared reading, rereading, and individual reading. Just as you do for other reading texts, you can use poems to point out features of text and reinforce reading skills you are teaching—as long as you focus first and primarily on the language and enjoyment of the whole poem.

My hope is that *Kids' Poems* has inspired you to write for and with your own students and to try poetry writing in your classroom. For other first-grade teachers and me, poetry writing has proved to be the easiest, most joyful, and most successful writing many first graders have ever done. I wish you the same ease, joy, and success.

Skating

I cerve
I jump
I tuerl
I can DO eny thing
I am Leping
thru the sky
a camol,
a sit spin,
a toelop,
a Haf flip,
I DO a split
I have the whol werdd
at my feet.

—BY CHRISTINA LEIGH SMITH

Skating

I curve
I jump
I twirl
I can do anything
I am leaping
through the sky
a camel
a sit spin
a toe loop
a half flip
I do a split
I have the whole world
at my feet.

—CHRISTINA LEIGH SMITH

41

FootBall

I Like

FootBall

I will

Never Cwit

tacaLing

Caching

Macing TuchDowns

Thats MY SPopst!

—BY KEENEN JOHN ATKINSON

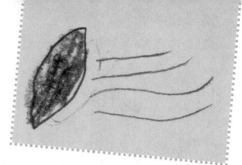

Football

I like

Football

I will

never quit

    tackling

catching

making touchdowns

That's MY SPORT!

—*KEENEN JOHN ATKINSON*

I do three terns

I do snow plows.

I do hocky stops.

I do T-stops.

I do crossovers. whew

I do Dabble loops.

I do thiple loops.

I do backwards crssoer
whew

finley I pass! a na the
level. whew

— BY ALEX HUANG

Never Give Up

I do three turns
I do snowplows
I do hockey stops
I do T-stops
Whew!

I do crossovers
I do double loops
I do triple loops
I do backwards crossovers
Whew!

Finally I pass!
Another level
Whew!

—ALEX HUANG

now Sol

nervous
sed
now Sol
hot wus
beati ng
fast
evewyn
wus lucing
at me
like I
wus Sesou

—BY GABRIELLE RACHEL HUGHLEY

46

New School

Nervous
scared
new school
Heart was
beating
fast
Everyone
was looking
at me
Like I
was special

—GABRIELLE RACHEL HUGHLEY

I run, he runs,
I wone, he last,
I dot lafe...
oh no, I dot,
I navr lafe al hnm,

—BY NOAH ECHOLS

Vinnie

I run, he runs.
I won, he lost.
I don't laugh...
Oh, no, I don't.
I never laugh at him.

—Noah Echols

Panda

The white and black mask face mov si 1"

~~mask face~~ moving

slowly throgh China.

Eating bamboo ~~as it~~

as it goes.

Meghan

— BY MEGHAN THOMPSON

Panda

The white and black face mask moving
slowly through China.
Eating bamboo
as it goes.

— *MEGHAN THOMPSON*

MARTIN LUThr KING

he is special
he isolvid problms
he madpefl happy and
he made countrez equal.

—BY MATTHEW MICHAEL LICINA

Martin Luther King

He is special.
He solved problems.
He made people happy
   and
he made countries
equal.

—MATTHEW MICHAEL LICINA

Only One ①

I'm the only one/
Without glasses,
Or contacs/
I hate being/
The Only One/
I'm the only,
Yongest/in my,
Family/ I hate
Being/the Only One,
I'm the Only
One/with fish

I hate being/

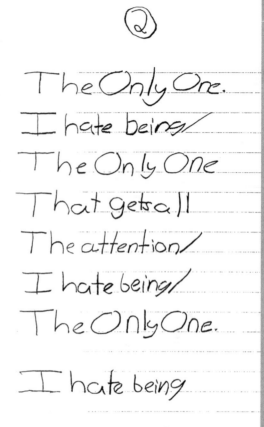

②

The Only One.
I hate being/
The Only One
That gets all
The attention/
I hate being/
The Only One.

I hate being

The Only One

—BY JOHN PAUL GORDON

Only One

I'm the only one
Without glasses
Or contacts
I hate being
The Only One

I'm the only,
Youngest
in my family
I hate being
The Only One

I'm the Only One
with fish
I hate being
The Only One

I hate being
The Only One
That gets all
The attention
I hate being
The Only One

I hate being
The Only One

—JOHN PAUL GORDON

55

My parents are seperated

1 I was eating

cereal
seareal 2 My Mom

said, 3 "We can't

to gether
live togther

4 any more!"

5 So were moving

6 My brother started

"crying!" → I just sat there

7 So we moved...

8 "I really

9 miss

10 my house."

11 "Anna moved

12 into my house."

its hard makeing a new hous your own.

—BY TESSA ROSE KEPNER-KRAUS

My Parents Are Separated

I was eating cereal.
My mom said,
"We can't live together
any more!"
So we're moving.
My brother started crying!
I just sat there.
So we moved...
"I really
miss
my house."
"Anna moved
into my house."
It's hard making
a new house
your own.

—TESSA ROSE KEPNER-KRAUS

MY CATS

two   cats

one hangs
^ one runs...
one dies one left
I miss that skiny
fellow.

—BY CECIE CULP

My Cats

two cats
one hangs
one runs…
one dies
one left
I miss that skinny fellow.

— CECIE CULP

59

I have Three dogs
one deid deid dead
howI have ToToTo
dogs dogs dos by by
by grchWuhe

—BY JAMES MICHAEL-PATRICK PHELAN

Gershwin

I have three dogs
one died, died, died

Now I have
two, two, two
dogs, dogs, dogs.

Bye bye,
Bye, Gershwin.

—JAMES MICHAEL-PATRICK PHELAN

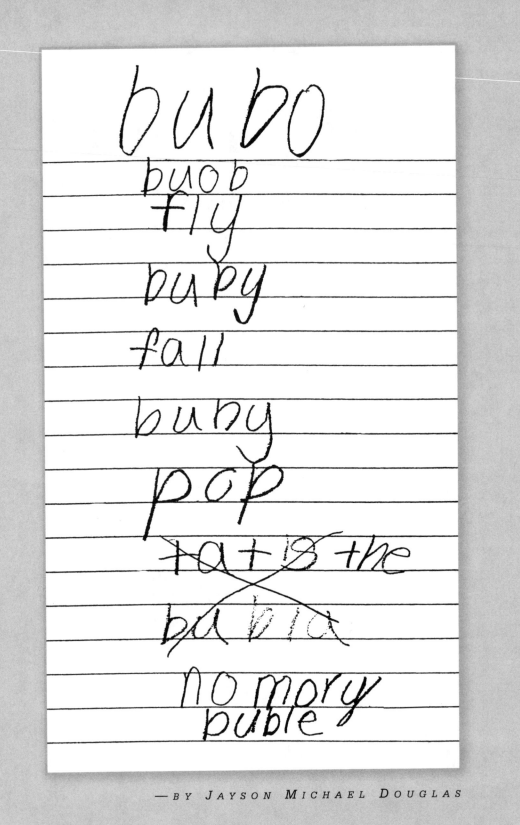

—BY JAYSON MICHAEL DOUGLAS

Bubbles

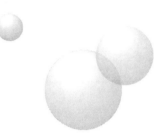

bubbles
fly
bubbles
fall
bubbles
pop
no more
bubble

—JAYSON MICHAEL DOUGLAS

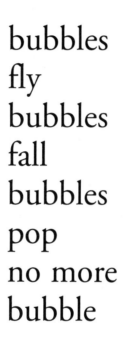

WirdLif

repling of wodr

anmis hodtig

wobling to Leve

crfoshing

hding fromdedng.

Bogs craplng ocosh
the foest foae.

Podrs sprsing era e
(setling)
Mther Nchen sloLy gtuing
estect Bycis of man

—BY KENNETH TOPPER LOCKWOOD

Wildlife

rippling of water
animals hunting
rustling of leaves
camouflaging
hiding from predators
bugs creeping across
the forest floor
predators surprising prey
Mother Nature slowly getting extinct
because of man

—KENNETH TOPPER
LOCKWOOD

A patern of my faverits
2-27-98

I don't like Ascparagis.

I like brocaley.

I don't like Spinig.

I like peenot boter and
Jelly.

I don't like tomatots.

I like Appels.

I don't like Sqac.

I like french tocte.

I don't like avacodos.

I like rice.

A Patern of my faveris

— BY SHANNON A. SHARKEY

▲▲▲▲▲▲▲▲▲▲▲▲▲▲▲▲▲▲▲▲▲▲▲▲▲▲▲

A Pattern of My Favorites

I don't like asparagus.
I like broccoli.
I don't like spinach.
I like peanut butter and jelly.
I don't like tomatoes.
I like apples.
I don't like squash.
I like French toast.
I don't like avocados.
I like rice.

A pattern of my favorites.

— SHANNON A. SHARKEY

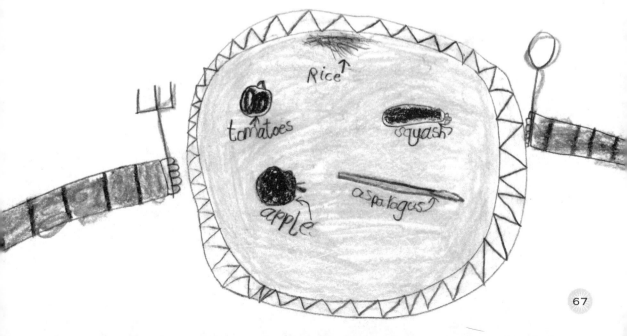

My family Likes
My sister

Likes the dog

My brother

dus To My

MoM Likes

flowers. My

DaD Likes

Bowling But

speshly they

Like Me.

—BY MIRIAM MOORE

My Family Likes

My sister
Likes the dog.
My brother
does too. My
Mom Likes
flowers. My
Dad Likes
Bowling. But
especially they
Like ME!

—MIRIAM MOORE

Grandma

Who is the one
who gives you candy?
Grandma.
Who is the one
who cares?
Grandma.
Who is the one
who pinches your/cheecks?
Grandma.

—BY KATRINA FORMAN

Grandma

Who is the one
who gives you candy?
Grandma.

Who is the one
who cares?
Grandma.

Who is the one
who pinches your
cheeks?
Grandma.

—*KATRINA FORMAN*

grandpa

grandpa was alve
now he is
i dead
I hope I can see him
up
in
hevin

—BY CARA WOOD

Grandpa

grandpa was alive.
now he is
    dead
I hope I can see him
    up
        in
            heaven.

—CARA WOOD

Mother's day

Mother day is when
mothers don't have
to do anything!
Because the kids do
most of the work and
the dads Just sit around

— BY CIARA I. HOLLAND

Mother's Day

Mother's Day is when
mothers don't have
to do anything!
Because the kids do
most of the work and
the dads just sit around.

—CIARA I. HOLLAND

My Brothers,

Sam is fun

Will is not

Sam is week

Will is Strg

but Both will

Bet me up.

Brothers, Brothers,
Brothers,

—BY ALEX FULTON

My Brothers

Sam is fun
Will is not
Sam is weak
Will is strong
But Both will
Beat me up.

Brothers, Brothers,
Brothers.

—ALEX FULTON

My baby Brother
My baby brother

craly craly craly
craly/ and drik
drik drik/ my mcm
call him a
gryley baby
because he drik
alite I love
my brother
scrach sctash
Twist twist
wiggly little
baby

lauth lauth
burp burp burp
happy
little baby

—BY RHANIYYAH A. WIMBERLY

My Baby Brother

Cry, cry, cry, cry
and drink, drink, drink.
My mom calls him a
greedy baby
because he drinks a lot.

I love my brother.

Scratch, scratch
twist, twist
wiggly little
baby.

Laugh, laugh
Burp, burp, burp
happy
Little baby.

— RHANIYYAH A.
WIMBERLY

Illustration Credits

Page 41: Kristen Sinicariello; *Page 43:* Adam Hershornin; *Page 45:* Emily Leirer;
Page 47: Augusta Funk; *Page 49:* Michael Rox; *Page 51:* Blake Jackson;
Page 53: Johnie Reed; *Page 55:* Leah Jones; *Page 57:* Ian Vitkus;
Page 59: Cheyla Robinson; *Page 61:* Firat Nurozler; Page 63: Harry Williams;
Page 65: Chloe Markewich; *Page 67:* Adam Hershorin;
Page 69: Katie DiVincenzo; *Page 71:* Emanuel Walker;
Page 73: Augusta Funk; *Page 75:* Kristen Sinicariello; *Page 77:* Katie DiVincenzo;
Page 79: Cortney Stiggers

Thanks also to:

Garrison Davis, Tyler Eiland, Jackie Genovese, Hattie Gemerchak, Tristian Hill,
Blake Jackson, Leah Jones, Tim Jones, Firat Nurozler, Johnie Reed,
Michael Rox, Kristen Sinicariello, Ian Vitkus, Emily Weatherhead,
Jennifer Weathers, Emanuel Walker, Harry Williams, Taylor Williams